eat your way to great SEX

LAGOON BOOKS

Project Editor: Sylvia Goulding

Book Design: Norma Martin

Thanks to Mike Goulding, Lesley Robb, Simon Farnhel, Ray Leaning, Nick Daws and
Ann Marangos

Cover Design: River Design. www.riverdesign.com

Series Editor: Lucy Dear
Visual concept: Sarah Wells
Based on original concept by Simon Melhuish

Published by:
LAGOON BOOKS
PO BOX 311, KT2 5QW, UK
PO BOX 990676, Boston, MA 02199, USA
www.lagoongames.com

ISBN: 1902813596

Printed in Hong Kong.

eat your way to

great

SEX

Introduction

Hey there! Is your sex life not all it could be? Don't worry—the solution is at hand! All the world's best lovers know this: great food leads to great sex. Our culinary Kama Sutra will show you the dishes to put you in the mood for some very adult fun and frolics...

First Base

In our opening chapter you'll find some sensual recipes to set the mood. Let the fragrance and taste of these delicious entrées, from *Half-Naked Asparagus Spears* to *Throw-your-Shirt-off Chili Squid*, arouse your baby's carnal lust. Soon they'll be looking at you with a fresh hunger...and full of anticipation of what is to come...

In the Mood for Love

Now you're both getting amorous, it's time to step up a gear. The main course recipes in this chapter have been hand-picked for their power to raise the erotic temperature. Savory dishes, from *Magic Mozzarella Beefcakes* to *Love-Smitten Lamb With Couscous*, will stimulate your lover's desires, and soon you'll be ready to get your fill of each other...

Late-night Lovin'

The midnight hour strikes, and we see you cuddled up, replete in the afterglow of a perfect meal. The taste-packed tempters in Chapter 3, from *Naughty Nutty Nibbles* to *Shrimps Wrapped in a Blanket*, will re-ignite the fires, so you'll scale even greater heights of passion!

Sweet Seduction

And finally, in Chapter 4, we present delicious desserts from *Nights in White Satin* to *Honey & Cream Figs*, to tantalize your senses, and to put you in the mood to fulfil those other sweet desires.

It's true! These fantastic recipes are all you need for a romantic night in with your true love. Each one will arouse fresh erotic anticipations, smoothly building the excitement from course to course, culminating in perfect, passionate fulfillment...

Great sex really will be yours on a plate!

chapter

chapter **2**

chapter **3**

chapter

First Base   p8

In the Mood for Love   p30

Late-night lovin'   p52

Sweet Seduction   p74

chapter

1

Tempt your lover with
these tantalizing tidbi

These aphrodisiac foods are guaranteed to put your honey in the mood for love...

contents

Smoldering Garlic Shrimps

Finger-Lickin' Artichoke Dippers

Spicy Red Pepper Soup

Shrimps in an Avocado Bed

Half-Naked Asparagus Spears

Throw-Your-Shirt-Off Chili Squid

Love-at-First-Bite Haddock Fingers

Seafood Spaghetti Serenade

Tantalizing Turkey Tagliatelle

Sizzling Stir-Fry Chicken

Smoldering Garlic Shrimps

Get passions rising with this steamy dish. These sizzling shrimps will light anyone's fire.

SERVES 2

What to buy

- 2 garlic cloves, finely chopped
- 1 small fresh chili, chopped
- 2 tbsp olive oil
- 150 g/5 oz shelled prawns (shrimps)
- Salt
- Parsley, finely chopped
- Lemon wedges and crusty bread to serve

How to cook it

1 Fry the garlic and chili in the oil. Add the shrimps as soon as the garlic begins to smolder. Do not allow the garlic to brown—it will make it taste bitter. Season with salt and continue to fry over a high heat for 1-2 minutes.

2 Sprinkle with parsley and serve sizzling hot, straight from the pan, with lemon wedges and crusty bread.

3 Enjoy the fiery flavor, and feel your lover's passions rise.

Finger-Lickin' Artichoke Dippers

For a perfect night in, start with these—they're tasty, hot and sure to please!

SERVES 2

What to buy

- 2 artichokes
- Salt
- Juice of ½ lemon

For the vinaigrette:
- 1 garlic clove, crushed
- 1 tsp mustard powder
- Juice of ½ lemon
- Salt and pepper
- 6 tbsp olive oil

How to cook it

1 Cut the stems off the artichokes close to the base. Bring a pan of salted water to the boil. Add the lemon juice and drop in the artichokes. Cover, turn down the heat and simmer for 40 minutes. Drain the artichokes upside down so that the water can run out.

❷ Meanwhile make the vinaigrette: stir the garlic and mustard into the lemon juice, season to taste, then stir in the oil and mix well to combine.

❸ To eat the artichokes, pull off the green leaves, one at a time. Dip the base of the leaf in the vinaigrette then eat the tender artichoke flesh. When you get to the artichoke heart, gently scrape off the fibrous choke and discard, drizzle the remaining vinaigrette over the heart and eat.

❹ Now you're ready for the main course—and the rest of the evening!

Artichokes, like wine, are good for the ladies—when gentlemen eat them...
(French Saying)

Exotic Pleasures

ARTICHOKES ARE A SENSUAL FOOD TO EAT TOGETHER AS YOU ARE USING YOUR FINGERS TO SLOWLY 'STRIP' THE PLANT OF ITS LEAVES. THESE EXOTIC LOOKING VEGETABLES ARE ALSO GOOD FOR YOU: THEY LOWER THE CHOLESTEROL LEVEL AND IMPROVE DIGESTION.

Spicy Red Pepper Soup

Get your sweetie blushing with this red-hot number. Peppery, yet smooth, it'll warm the blood on the coolest night.

SERVES 6

What to buy

- 2 red (bell) peppers, seeded
- 3 tbsp oil
- ½ tsp fresh marjoram, chopped
- 1 garlic clove, crushed
- 1 tsp mild curry paste
- ½ red onion, sliced
- ½ leek, sliced
- 125 g/4½ oz green cabbage, chopped
- 3 tomatoes, peeled, quartered and seeded
- 1 tsp sweet chili sauce
- Salt and pepper

How to cook it

❶ Grill the peppers, skin side uppermost, until the skin blackens and blisters. Allow to cool a little, then slip off the skins.

❷ Heat the oil in a large saucepan, add the herbs, the garlic, and the curry paste. Stir over a low heat for about 1 minute.

❸ Add the onion and leek, and cook for a further 3 minutes. Add the cabbage, tomatoes, (bell) peppers, and about 1 liter/35 fl oz water. Bring to the boil, then reduce the heat, cover the saucepan, and simmer for

for about 20 minutes. Remove from the heat and allow to cool slightly.

4 Purée the soup in a food processor or with a hand-held blender. Add the chili sauce and season to taste. Freeze two-thirds of the soup, so you'll always have some ready.

5 Reheat gently when you are ready. Serve with a glass of chilled white wine, such as Chardonnay, for a delicious, contrasting taste.

Soup and fish explain
half the emotions of
human life...
(Sidney Smith)

Vitamin power

PEPPERS BELONG TO THE SAME BOTANICAL FAMILY AS CHILIES, AND THEY SHARE MANY OF THEIR HOTTER COUSINS' LOVE REPUTATION. THEY'RE ALSO RICH IN VITAMINS A AND C, WHICH WILL GIVE YOU A SMOOTH, SEXY SKIN, BRIGHT LOVIN' EYES, AND GENERAL GOOD HEALTH AND STAMINA.

Shrimps in an Avocado Bed

A succulent starter of shameless desires. Plump shrimps to be sucked and savored on a bed of sin!

SERVES 2

What to buy

- 100 g/4 oz large fresh prawns (shrimps)
- 1 red chili
- 3 tbsp olive oil
- 2 garlic cloves, crushed
- Salt and pepper
- 1 avocado
- 2 tbsp mayonnaise

How to cook it

1 Remove the heads and shells from the prawns (shrimps), leaving the tails intact. Halve the chili lengthwise and discard the seeds.

2 Heat the oil in a pan. Add all the prawns (shrimps), chili and garlic and cook over a high heat for about 3 minutes, stirring, until the prawns (shrimps) turn pink. Season with salt and pepper to taste.

3 Meanwhile, halve the avocado lengthways and remove the stone.
4 When the prawns (shrimps) are cooked, remove them from the pan and pat dry with kitchen paper. Stir in the mayonnaise, then divide them equally between the two avocado halves and serve. Make sure you tell your lover what this dish is called!

Food and Sex.
Basic desires.
Can't avoid them...
(From the film Tampopo)

So good together

PRAWNS (SHRIMPS), LIKE MOST OTHER SEAFOOD, CONTAIN HIGH LEVELS OF ZINC WHICH IS SAID TO ENHANCE THE SEX DRIVE. AND THE NAME OF THE EXQUISITELY SMOOTH AVOCADO DERIVES FROM THE AZTEC WORD 'AHUACACUAHATL,' MEANING TESTICLE TREE!

Half-Naked Asparagus Spears

**Get your baby in the mood for love with these shameless vegetables—
the more tender, the better!**

SERVES 2

What to buy

- A bunch of fresh green
  or white asparagus spears
- Salt
- 4 rashers (strips) bacon

For the vinaigrette:
- 1 garlic clove, crushed
- 1 tsp Dijon mustard
- 1 tbsp balsamic vinegar
- Salt and pepper
- 6 tbsp virgin olive oil

How to cook it

❶ Cut off the woody end of the asparagus spears. Using white kitchen string, tie the spears into a bundle so that they will stand on end. Bring a tall pan of salted water to the boil, stand the spears upright in the pan, tips uppermost. Cover the pan with a

18

foil dome and seal as tightly as possible. Simmer for 10-30 minutes, depending on the size of the spears, until they are cooked. Use a sharp knife to check the asparagus is done: it should easily pierce the stems.

2 Meanwhile make the vinaigrette by mixing together all the ingredients. Heat the grill to high.

3 When the asparagus is cooked, remove the foil, and carefully take the spears out of the water. Wrap bacon around each spear, and place under the grill until the bacon is cooked.

4 Put on a slow, smoochy record, and serve immediately, with the vinaigrette dressing and crusty bread to mop up the juices.

You needn't tell me that a man who doesn't love oysters and asparagus and good wines has got a soul... (Saki)

Shapely vegetable

THE APHRODISIAC PROPERTIES OF ASPARAGUS WERE ALREADY KNOWN TO THE GREEKS AND ROMANS, WHO COLLECTED IT WILD ON THE HILLSIDES. A VEGETABLE HIGH IN VITAMIN A AND PHOSPHORUS, KING LOUIS XIV PROBABLY ALSO KNEW ABOUT ITS SECRET—HE JUST COULDN'T GET ENOUGH OF IT!

Throw-Your-Shirt-Off Chili Squid

This fishy feast will raise the temperature—time to shed a few of those garments?

SERVES 2

What to buy

- 4 large dried anchos chilies
- ½ onion, chopped
- 4 small hot chili peppers, chopped
- 1 tbsp vegetable oil
- 2 garlic cloves, crushed
- 400 g/14 oz can chopped tomatoes
- 125 ml/4 fl oz/½ cup dry white wine
- 1 tsp dried oregano
- ½ tsp ground cumin
- ½ tsp ground coriander (cilantro)
- 1 small bay leaf
- 225 g/8 oz fresh baby squid, uncooked
- Salt and pepper
- Fresh coriander (cilantro), chopped
- Lime wedges, to garnish

How to cook it

❶ In a saucepan, cover the anchos with water and bring to the boil. Take off the heat and leave for 10 minutes.

❷ Meanwhile, in a large pot heat the oil and fry the onion and hot chili peppers for 5 minutes, or until soft. Add the garlic and cook for another minute. Stir in the tomatoes, wine, oregano, cumin, coriander (cilantro), and bay leaf. Bring to the boil, reduce the heat, cover, and simmer for 15 minutes.

3 Meanwhile, drain, skin, and seed the anchos. Blend with a ladle of the tomato mixture, then return to the pot and simmer for a further 15 minutes.

4 Stir the squid into the sauce. Cook for 2 minutes. Season to taste. Serve with coriander (cilantro), and limes.

5 Watch the steam rise and be prepared for some serious lovin'.

Next to jazz music, there is nothing that lifts the spirit and strengthens the soul more than a good bowl of chili...
(Harry James)

Too hot to handle

THE MEXICAN HABAÑERO AND THE CARIBBEAN SCOTCH BONNET SHARE THE HONOR OF BEING THE WORLD'S HOTTEST CHILIES. BOTH ARE SHAPED LIKE LANTERNS AND ARE ABOUT AS LARGE AS A WALNUT. THE SEEDS AND WHITE MEMBRANES ARE THE HOTTEST PARTS. AVOID TOUCHING THESE, OR WEAR RUBBER GLOVES —THEY MAY CAUSE SERIOUS PAIN!

Love-at-First-Bite Haddock Fingers

Savor them, fondle them, devour them—you know you want to, so why resist?

SERVES 2

What to buy

- 225 g/½ lb haddock fillets, skinned
- 1 small egg
- 25 g/1 oz fresh breadcrumbs
- 1 tbsp fresh coriander (cilantro) finely chopped
- 1 tsp ground cumin
- Salt and pepper
- Vegetable oil for frying
- Mayonnaise
- Lime wedges

How to cook it

1 Cut the haddock fillets into bite-sized pieces.

2 Beat the egg on a plate. On a second plate, spread out the bread-crumbs, mix in the coriander (cilantro) and cumin, then season

to taste with salt and pepper.
Turn the fish pieces first in the egg,
then in the breadcrumb mixture to
coat evenly all over.

3 Heat the oil in a frying pan and
fry the fish for about 5-10 minutes, or
until golden, turning once. Drain on
kitchen paper.

4 Serve the fish fingers with mayo
for dipping, and lime wedges to
squeeze all over them. Let the
chemistry work—gaze into each
other's eyes and feel yourselves falling
deeper and deeper in love.

Sharing food with
another human being is
an intimate act that
should not be indulged
in lightly...
(M. F. K. Fisher)

Erotic Creatures

FISH, PACKED WITH
PHOSPHATES AND IODINE, IS
BELIEVED TO BE A POWERFUL
EROTIC AID. WHEN THE
ROMAN POET AUSONIUS
WROTE A LOVE POEM FOR THE
MOSELLE RIVER, HE DEVOTED
150 OF HIS VERSES TO FISH!

Seafood Spaghetti Serenade

Show your baby how much you care with this melodious ménage of pasta, seafood, and tomatoes.

SERVES 2

What to buy

- 225 g/½ lb fresh clams, cleaned
- 100 g/4 oz tomatoes
- 3 tbsp olive oil
- 1 garlic clove, crushed
- 225 g/½ lb spaghetti
- Salt and pepper
- ½ tbsp fresh parsley, chopped

How to cook it

❶ Place the clams in a large pan of water, and cook until the shells open, then remove the clams from the shells. Discard any clams that did not open. Strain the cooking liquid and reserve for later.

❷ Plunge the tomatoes into boiling water for 1 minute, then slip off the skins. Halve the tomatoes, and remove the seeds.

3 Heat the oil in a heavy pan, add the garlic and simmer gently for 2 minutes. Add the tomatoes and mash with the back of a spoon. Pour in the reserved clam water, stir to combine, and simmer for about 20 minutes.

4 Meanwhile cook the spaghetti according to instructions. Drain.

5 Add the clams and parsley to the tomato sauce and heat for about 1 minute. Stir the sauce into the spaghetti and toss well.

6 Serve, to the sound of Neapolitan love songs, and your sweetheart is sure to go weak at the knees.

It's difficult to think anything but pleasant thoughts while eating a homegrown tomato... (Lewis Grizzard)

Pick your poison

TOMATOES, FEATURING PROMINENTLY IN MANY OF TODAY'S DISHES, WERE ONCE FEARED TO BE POISONOUS! THEY HAD A REPUTATION FOR CAUSING GOUT, CANCER, AND EXCESSIVE SEXUAL APPETITE— WHICH IS PROBABLY WHY THEY WERE ALSO KNOWN AS 'LOVE APPLES' IN FRANCE.

Tantalizing Turkey Tagliatelle

Drive your lover wild with succulent strips of meat in an aromatic pasta sauce. They'll be begging you for more!

SERVES 2

What to buy

- 1 turkey breast, skinned
- 1 ½ tbsp olive oil
- Salt and pepper
- 2 tomatoes, skinned
- 225 ml/8 fl oz/ ½ cup dry white wine
- 2 anchovy fillets, drained and chopped
- 2 garlic cloves, crushed
- A small handful of fresh basil, chopped
- ¼ tsp fresh oregano, chopped
- 225g/ 8oz tagliatelle
  or other pasta shapes
- 50g /2oz stoned black olives, sliced
- Grated Parmesan cheese

How to cook it

① Cut the turkey breast into bite-sized strips. Heat the oil in a frying pan over medium heat. Add the turkey strips and fry over a high heat for about 5 minutes. Turn the strips over, season, and cook for a further 5 minutes. Remove the turkey from pan and set aside.

2 Halve and seed the tomatoes, then chop the flesh. Add the wine to the hot pan and cook for 2 minutes over a high heat. Add the anchovies, garlic, basil, oregano, and the tomatoes. Stir to combine and cook for 20 minutes over a low heat.

3 Meanwhile, cook the tagliatelle according to instructions. Drain.

4 Return the turkey to the sauce and simmer for 3 minutes over low heat. Stir in the hot tagliatelle and the olives, then simmer for another 3 minutes. Check the seasoning.

5 Serve with a bowl of grated Parmesan cheese to sprinkle over the pasta, and taste the temptation.

Revvin' up

DO YOU SOMETIMES FIND THAT YOU (OR YOUR BABY) ARE SIMPLY NOT IN THE MOOD FOR LOVE? THIS COULD BE BECAUSE YOUR SYSTEM IS LOW ON SERATONIN, ENERGY, AND DRIVE. A PASTA FEAST SUCH AS THIS ONE PROVIDES AN EASY INSTANT CARBO FIX—YOU'LL SOON NOTICE THE DIFFERENCE!

Sizzling Stir-Fry Chicken

Inflame your lover's passions with this red-hot recipe. Don't serve too much, or you may have to go straight to the main course!

SERVES 2

What to buy

- 1 tbsp groundnut oil
- 1 garlic clove, crushed
- 1 cm/½ in piece fresh ginger, grated
- 1 red chili, seeded and chopped
- 1 chicken breast, skinned
- 100 g/4 oz carrots, cut into batons
- 100 g/4 oz broccoli, cut into florets
- 100 g/4 oz shitake mushrooms, sliced
- 100 g/4 oz mangetout (snowpeas), sliced lengthways
- 1 tbsp dark soy sauce
- 1 tbsp dry sherry
- 5 tbsp vegetable stock
- 1 tsp cornflour (cornstarch)
- 75 g/3 oz beansprouts
- 1 tbsp sesame seeds, toasted

How to cook it

❶ Heat the oil in a wok or large frying pan until it lightly begins to smoke. Add the garlic, ginger, and chili and stir fry for 1 minute. Add the chicken strips and continue frying for a further 5 minutes until the chicken has taken on color.

2 Add the carrots and broccoli and stir-fry continuously for 1-2 minutes.

3 Next add the mushrooms and mangetout (snowpeas), and continue stir-frying for a further 2-3 minutes.

4 Add the soy sauce, sherry, and stock, and bring to the boil. Mix the cornflour (cornstarch) with a little water to make a smooth paste. Stir in and cook for 1 minute.

5 Remove from the heat and quickly stir in the beansprouts and sesame seeds. Check the seasoning.

6 Serve with a hot cup of sake, to fan the flames of passion.

Gingerly does it

GINGER, AN ESSENTIAL PART OF MANY STIR-FRIES, WAS DESCRIBED AS AN APHRODISIAC IN THE ANCIENT ARABIC EROTIC HANDBOOK 'THE PERFUMED GARDEN'—MEN ARE PROMISED THAT, IF THEY CHEWED A GINGER AND CINNAMON MIXTURE, 'SHE WILL HAVE SUCH AFFECTION FOR YOU THAT SHE CAN SCARCELY BE A MOMENT WITHOUT YOU…'

chapter 2

In th

**Red-hot meals for
love-hungry
guys and gals**

Now you've set the scene, make sure you get mind and body ready for things to come...

contents

Tasty Tomato Soup — 33

Wickedly Wonderful Wings — 34

Saucy Spaghetti Puttanesca — 36

Sinful Sausages & Beans — 38

Steamy Salmon Crêpes — 40

Temptin' Tuna Noodles — 42

Red Hot Pork Chili — 44

Magic Mozzarella Beefcakes — 46

Lusty Lamb with Couscous — 48

Fervent Fish Curry — 50

Tasty Tomato Soup

Titillate your lover's taste-buds with this steamy, creamy love-apple soup.

SERVES 2

What to buy

- 15 g/½ oz butter
- 2 small potatoes, peeled and cubed
- 1 carrot, chopped
- 1 small onion, finely chopped
- 1 garlic clove, crushed
- 225 g/8 oz can tomatoes
- 150 ml/5 fl oz hot vegetable stock
- 1 tsp fresh basil, chopped
- 1 tsp sugar
- Salt and pepper

How to cook it

1 Heat the butter in a saucepan, add the potatoes, carrot, onion, and garlic, and gently fry for 5 minutes to soften. Add the tomatoes with their juice and half the stock, stirring to break up the tomatoes. Bring to the boil.

2 Add the basil and sugar, and season. Reduce the heat, cover and simmer gently for about 20 minutes, or until the vegetables are tender.

3 Whizz the soup with a hand-held blender to give a rough purée. Add as much stock as needed to make the soup as thick or liquid as you like.

4 Heat through and serve with plenty of crusty bread.

Wickedly Wonderful Wings

**Irresistibly good, these tasty chicken wings will set you on fire—
better keep a chilled beer handy before you burn up!**

SERVES 2

What to buy

- 2 tsp vegetable oil
- ½ onion, very finely chopped
- 1 garlic clove, crushed
- 1 tbsp clear honey
- 2 tbsp tomato ketchup
- 2 tbsp Worcestershire sauce
- 1 tsp mustard
- 1 tsp chili sauce
- 4 chicken wings
- 1 tbsp flour
- Salt and pepper

How to cook it

1 Heat the oven to 200°C/400°F/ Gas Mark 6. Heat the oil in a small pan, add the onion and garlic and fry for 5 minutes, or until softened. Stir in the honey, ketchup, Worcestershire sauce, mustard, and chili sauce. Cover and simmer gently for 1-2 minutes.

❷ Put the flour on a plate and season with salt and pepper. Turn chicken in the seasoned flour to coat evenly, then brush liberally with the sauce from the pan. Place chicken wings on a baking tray and cook in the oven for about 30 minutes, or until browned and cooked through.

❸ Serve piping hot, and keep the number of the fire brigade handy, in case the flames get out of hand.

The way to a man's heart is through his stomach...
(Fanny Fern)

Finger-lickin' good

RICH IN VITAMIN B, ENZYMES AND AMINO ACIDS, HONEY—USED TO GLAZE THE WINGS—IS A GREAT LOVE FOOD. IN SOME CULTURES, BRIDE AND GROOM HAVE THEIR PALMS SPREAD WITH HONEY. LICKING IT OFF EACH OTHER, THEY BELIEVE, ENSURES A SWEET LIFE TOGETHER. NOW THERE'S AN IDEA...

Saucy Spaghetti Puttanesca

Those Italians knew a thing or two about love—the saucy capers in this Mediterranean classic will set the tone for later!

SERVES 2

What to buy

- 250 g/9 oz spaghetti or other pasta shapes
- Salt

For the puttanesca sauce:
- 1 tbsp olive oil
- 2 garlic cloves, finely chopped
- 1 red chili, seeded and chopped
- 2 anchovies, rinsed and drained
- 100 g/4 oz black or green olives, stoned and chopped
- 1 tbsp capers, rinsed and drained
- 225 g /8 oz can chopped tomatoes
- 1 tbsp tomato purée
- A small handful fresh basil, chopped
- A small handful fresh oregano, chopped
- Pepper

To serve:
- Crusty bread and grated Parmesan cheese

How to cook it

❶ Make the sauce: heat the oil in a saucepan, then add the garlic and chili, and cook for about 5 minutes, or until the garlic is beginning to take on color.

❷ Add all the other ingredients, stir and season to taste with pepper. Turn the heat to low, cover, and simmer for about 30 minutes.

❸ Meanwhile, cook the pasta according to packet instructions and drain. Return pasta to the pan, then pour the sauce over the pasta. Mix thoroughly.

❹ Serve with crusty bread and fresh Parmesan cheese, and dream of making *amore* under star-lit Mediterranean skies.

Breath-taking!

ONE OF THE OLDEST PLANTS IN CULTIVATION, GARLIC IS KNOWN AS 'FOOD OF LOVE'. ODYSSEUS, ON HIS JOURNEY HOME FROM TROY, WAS HELD CAPTIVE BY THE WITCH CIRCE, WHO TRIED TO BEWITCH HIM WITH LOVE POTIONS. ODYSSEUS, HOWEVER, WAS PARTIAL TO GARLIC, WHICH MADE HIM IMMUNE TO THE POTIONS, WHILE CIRCE HERSELF FELL IN LOVE WITH ODYSSEUS!

Sinful Sausages & Beans

Gird your loins with this protein-packed feast—you'll be needing them later!

SERVES 2
What to buy

- 4 tbsp vegetable oil
- 100 g/4 oz lean, rindless bacon, chopped
- ½ onion, chopped
- 1 tbsp fresh sage, chopped
- 1 sprig of rosemary
- 1 garlic clove, crushed
- 400 g/14 oz can black beans, drained
- 1 celery stalk, chopped
- 2 bay leaves
- 225 g/8 oz can chopped tomatoes
- ½ chicken stock cube
- 3 tbsp red wine
- Salt and pepper
- 4 spicy sausages

How to cook it

① Heat 3 tbsp of the oil in a large saucepan, add bacon, onion, herbs, and garlic and fry for 5 minutes, or until the onion is beginning to color.

❷ Add the black beans, celery, and bay leaves. Stir well. Simmer gently for 10 minutes to allow the flavors to mingle, then add the tomatoes and crumble in the stock cube. Add 2 tbsp of the wine, season to taste, stir, cover and simmer gently for about 30 minutes to thicken.

❸ Meanwhile, in a small frying pan, heat the remaining oil. Add the sausages and fry over a low heat for 20 minutes, turning occasionally.

❹ Transfer the cooked sausages to warm serving plates, and add a good portion of the beans to each one. Pour the remaining wine into the frying pan, scrape out the cooking juices, and pour over the beans. Serve piping hot, and freeze any left-over beans for your lover's next visit.

Energy Packs

BEANS ARE A FANTASTIC SOURCE OF IRON, ZINC, POTASSIUM, AND MAGNESIUM, AND AS SUCH WILL PROTECT YOU FROM ALL SORTS OF DISEASES. PERHAPS EVEN MORE IMPORTANTLY, THEY WILL ALSO IMPROVE YOUR PERFORMANCE, INCREASE YOUR STAMINA, AND GIVE YOU PLENTY OF SPARE ENERGY...

Steamy Salmon Crêpes

Smooth, succulent, sensual, these crêpes are just right to set you up for some heavy necking.

MAKES 8

What to buy

- 125 g/4 ½ oz plain (all-purpose) flour
- Salt
- 1 egg
- 600 ml/1 pint/20 fl oz milk
- Vegetable oil for frying
- 350 g/12 oz smoked salmon
- 1 bay leaf
- ½ onion, sliced
- 40 g/1 ½ oz butter
- 150 ml/¼ pint/5 fl oz single (light) cream
- 2 eggs, hard boiled, shelled and chopped
- 3 tbsp fresh parsley, chopped
- Fresh chives, snipped, to garnish

How to cook it

❶ Sift 100 g/4 oz of the flour and a pinch of salt into a bowl. Break in the egg. Gradually add a quarter of the milk and beat until you have a thick, smooth batter. Add a further quarter of milk and beat until smooth.

❷ Heat a little oil in a frying pan and when it is very hot, pour in a small amount of batter. Tip the pan quickly so the batter covers the bottom of the pan. Cook over a high heat until the underside is golden brown, then turn over and cook the other side. Cook eight crêpes and keep warm.

❸ Place the salmon in a saucepan, pour over the remaining milk and add the bay leaf and onion. Cover the pan and simmer for 5 minutes, or until the fish begins to flake. Strain off and reserve the milk. Flake the fish.

❹ Heat the oven to 200°C/400°F/Gas Mark 6. Melt the butter in a pan, stir in the remaining flour and cook for 1 minute, stirring. Remove the pan from the heat and gradually stir in the reserved milk. Bring to the boil and cook, stirring, until sauce thickens.

❺ Off the heat, stir in cream, fish, chopped egg, and parsley. Season to taste and allow to cool slightly.

❻ Divide the fish mixture equally between the crêpes, fold over and place in individual dishes or one large ovenproof dish. Cover with foil and cook in the oven for about 20 minutes.

Feelin' special

SALMON, OFTEN CONSIDERED A LUXURY FOOD, TASTES AND LOOKS EXTRA SPECIAL IN THESE DELICIOUS CRÊPES. SERVE THEM WITH CHAMPAGNE, WHICH IS THOUGHT TO BE THE MOST EFFECTIVE APHRODISIAC OF ALL ALCOHOLIC DRINKS— THE BUBBLES WILL STIMULATE THE PALATE, AND THE ALCOHOL MAKES YOU FEEL RELAXED AND UNINHIBITED...

❼ Scatter over the remaining chives to garnish, and serve with chilled Champagne.

Temptin' Tuna Noodles

This tasty, Japanese-style dish is full of Eastern promise. Noodles will soon turn to canoodles!

SERVES 2

What to buy

- 1 garlic clove, crushed
- ½ tsp wasabi paste
- 1 tsp cornflour (cornstarch)
- 2 tbsp Japanese soy sauce
- 2 fresh tuna steaks, each cut into four pieces
- 125 g/5 oz Japanese noodles
- 1 ½ tbsp vegetable oil
- 1 small red (bell) pepper, seeded and thinly sliced
- 4 spring onions (scallions), cut into short lengths
- 50 g/2 oz shiitake mushrooms
- 375 ml/12 fl oz fish stock
- 1 sheet nori seaweed, cut into thin strips

How to cook it

❶ Mix the garlic, wasabi, cornflour (cornstarch), and 1tbsp soy sauce. Spread over the tuna. Cook noodles according to packet instructions.

❷ In a wok or large frying pan, heat 1 tbsp oil, and stir-fry the (bell) pepper, spring onions (scallions) and mushrooms for 3-4 minutes. Lift out with a slotted spoon.

❸ Brush a heavy-based frying pan with a little of the remaining oil and heat until very hot. Cook the tuna for 2 minutes each side, until just cooked.

❹ Pour in the stock and the remaining soy sauce. Add the noodles, vegetables, and seaweed and toss well.

❺ Transfer noodles and vegetables to two hot serving plates, top with tuna and spoon over the sauce.

❻ Savor the flavor, and the sultry mood that is sure to ensue.

One cannot think well, love well, sleep well, if one has not dined well...
(Virginia Woolf)

Keep going

FISH IS VERY RICH IN PHOSPHORUS, WHICH WAS ALREADY KNOWN TO 19TH-CENTURY FRENCH DOCTORS AS A POWERFUL SEXUAL STIMULANT. COMBINE THE ENERGY-GIVING PROPERTIES OF CARBO-RICH PASTA WITH THE INVIGORATING EFFECT OF TUNA, AND THERE'S NO TELLING WHAT MAY HAPPEN...

Red Hot Pork Chili

If you can't stand the heat, stay out of the chili! This rampant recipe will have you panting for more.

SERVES 2

What to buy

- 2 tbsp vegetable oil
- 225 g/8 oz pork, diced
- 1 onion
- 3 garlic cloves, crushed
- 3-4 fresh chilies, seeded and chopped
- 1 tbsp paprika
- 400 g/14 oz can kidney beans, drained
- 225 g/8 oz can tomatoes
- 1 tbsp tomato purée
- Salt and pepper
- 1 red (bell) pepper

How to cook it

❶ In a large ovenproof casserole dish, heat the oil, and fry the pork on all sides for about 5 minutes, or until browned all over. Lift out with a slotted spoon and keep warm.

❷ Heat the oven to 170°C/325°F/ Gas Mark 3. Add the onions, garlic, and chilies, and fry for 5 minutes, stirring occasionally, until softened. Return the meat to the casserole.

❸ Add the paprika and cook for 2-3 minutes. Add the beans and the tomatoes with their juices, the tomato purée, and season to taste. Stir well to mix. Cover and cook in the oven for about 1 hour.

4 Halve and seed the (bell) pepper, then cut into strips. Add the pepper strips to the casserole, stir, and return to the oven for another 30 minutes, or until the meat is well done.

5 Check the seasoning, turn the lights down low, and serve with a bowl of fluffy rice.

Wish I had time for just one more bowl of chili... (the dying words of Kit Carson)

Magic Mozzarella Beefcakes

Cast a spell with these bewitching burgers. Your baby will be powerless to resist their Italian charm!

SERVES 2

What to buy

- 1 small onion, chopped
- 225 g/8 oz lean minced (ground) beef
- 1 egg
- 3 tbsp fresh breadcrumbs
- 2 tsp fresh marjoram, chopped
- 2 tsp tomato purée
- Salt and pepper
- 4 slices of mozzarella cheese
- 4 buns
- 4 large tomato slices

How to cook it

❶ In a large bowl, combine the onion, beef, egg, breadcrumbs, marjoram, and tomato purée. Season to taste, and mix well. Divide the mixture into 4 equal portions and press into burger shapes.

❷ Heat the grill to high. Place the burgers on a baking tray and cook

46

under the grill for 12-15 minutes, or until evenly cooked, turning once.

❸ Halve the buns and place under the grill for a couple of minutes while the burgers are cooking, to toast them. Place the burgers on the bottom halves of the buns, place a slice of mozzarella cheese on each one, and return to the grill for 1 minute, or until the cheese begins to melt.

❹ Top the cheeseburgers with tomato slices and the top half of the buns. Serve with a glass of Chianti, and make sure you leave the phone off the hook, so you won't be interrupted.

A dinner which ends without cheese is like a beautiful woman with only one eye...
(A. Brillat-Savarin)

Buffalo Bill

THIS ITALIAN-STYLE BURGER IS MADE WITH MOZZARELLA, AN ESSENTIAL INGREDIENT IN ALL PIZZAS, MADE FROM BUFFALO MILK. THERE ARE CHEESES MADE FROM THE MILK OF MARES, ZEBRAS, REINDEER, LLAMAS, AND YAKS. ASS'S MILK, HOWEVER, CLEOPATRA'S BATH ADDITIVE, HAS NEVER BEEN MADE INTO CHEESE...

Lusty Lamb with Couscous

Moroccan magic! These tender morsels in a bed of fluffy couscous will get your lover in the mood for a steamy night.

SERVES 2

What to buy

- 150 g/5 oz lamb fillet
- 1 tbsp olive oil
- 1 ½ tbsp fresh parsley, rosemary, and mint, chopped
- 1 tbsp fresh white breadcrumbs
- Salt and pepper
- 75 g/3 oz couscous
- 1 tbsp toasted pine kernels
- 150 ml/5 fl oz hot vegetable stock
- Juice of ½ lemon

How to cook it

❶ Heat the oven to 190°C/375°F/ Gas Mark 5. Cut the lamb into large pieces and brush all over with a little oil. In a small bowl, combine the herbs and breadcrumbs and season. Turn the lamb in the mixture to coat well. Transfer the meat to a roasting tin, drizzle over the remaining oil and cook for about 30 minutes in the oven, or until tender.

❷ Ten minutes before the lamb is cooked, put the couscous and pine kernels into a bowl. Pour over the vegetable stock and lemon juice. Leave to stand, in a warm place, for 7 minutes, then fluff up with a fork.

❸ Transfer the lamb to hot serving plates and serve with the couscous.

❹ Now slip into a sexy little number, leave the door ajar and ask your honey to help themselves...

Lust isn't all there is to sex. Sex isn't all there is to love. But love is almost all there is to life...
(Eddie Cantor)

Pining for love

MANY MIDDLE EASTERN DISHES COMBINE MEAT WITH FRUIT AND NUTS. THE PINE KERNELS IN THIS RECIPE ARE KNOWN AS POWERFUL LOVE AGENTS—AN ANCIENT EROTIC TEXT SUGGESTS THAT MEN SHOULD TAKE A GLASSFUL OF THICK HONEY, 20 ALMONDS, AND 100 PINE KERNELS FOR THREE NIGHTS BEFORE BED, TO INCREASE THEIR VIGOR...

Fervent Fish Curry

This tumultuous recipe is a treat for all the senses—and will raise the pulse for what is to follow...

SERVES 2

What to buy

- 2 garlic cloves, crushed
- 2.5 cm/1 in fresh root ginger, peeled and finely chopped
- 1 fresh red chili, seeded and chopped
- Salt
- 350 g/12 oz cod fillets, skinned
- 50 g/2 oz chick pea flour
- ½ tsp red chili powder
- ½ tsp ground turmeric
- 1 tsp ground coriander (cilantro)
- 1 tsp ground cumin
- ½ tsp fresh thyme
- 2 tsp garam masala
- 2 tbsp fresh mint, finely chopped
- 2 tbsp vegetable oil

How to cook it

❶ In a large bowl, combine the garlic, ginger, and chili with ½ tsp salt and a little water to make a paste. Cut fish into bite-sized pieces, place into the bowl and coat with the paste. Leave to marinate for 1-2 hours.

❷ Put the chick pea flour on a large shallow dish. Season with salt, chili powder, turmeric, coriander thyme, half the garam masala and half the fresh mint. Mix well to combine.

❸ Heat the oil in a large frying pan. Remove the cod from the marinade, and turn in the seasoned flour until well coated. Put the fish into the pan and fry for about 5-10 minutes until it is crisp and golden.

❹ Transfer the fish to serving plates and garnish with the remaining garam masala and fresh mint.

❺ Serve with steaming rice and a fresh salad—and watch your baby's last efforts at resistance melt away.

I've had sex and I've had food, and I'd rather eat... (Florence King)

chapter 3

Midnight snacks and love potions to p[ut] you in the mood

52

Late-night Lovin'

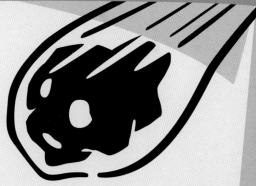

Get a mouthful of these tasty bites to restore your energies and keep you going...

contents

Baked Love Oysters

Sexy Salmon Sushi

Shrimps wrapped in a Blanket

Silky Smooth Dip

Pep-up-your-Lovelife Pizza

Frisky Frittata with Peppers

Creamy Venison Goulash

Naughty Nutty Nibbles

Passionate Potions

Bedtime Beverages

Baked Love Oysters

Succulent oysters in a sensual salsa sauce. Your baby will be begging you for more!

SERVES 2

What to buy

- 1 large ripe tomato
- 2 tbsp lime juice
- ½ red onion, diced
- 2 tsp fresh coriander (cilantro), chopped
- 2 fresh hot green chilies (preferably jalapeño), diced
- 1 garlic clove, crushed
- A pinch of salt
- 12 fresh oysters

How to cook it

1 Make a salsa: skin and chop the tomato, add the remaining ingredients bar the oysters, cover and chill in the refrigerator.

2 Heat the oven to 240°C/475°F/Gas Mark 9. Place the oysters on a baking sheet and bake for about 3-5 minutes, or until just opened.

3 Arrange the oysters on two large plates. Serve with the salsa, and get ready to get up close and personal with your baby.

Sexy Salmon Sushi

Rekindle the flames of your passion with these exotic morsels—the night is young and there's still more frolicking fun to be had!

SERVES 2

What to buy

- 175 g/6 oz sushi rice
- 2 tbsp rice wine vinegar
- 1 ½ tbsp caster (superfine) sugar
- A pinch of salt
- 150 g/5 oz skinned salmon fillet, cut into slices
- Wasabi paste

How to cook it

❶ Rinse the rice under cold water, drain, cover with water in a saucepan and bring to the boil. Cover and cook over a low heat for 15 minutes until the water is absorbed. Leave to stand for 15 minutes; transfer to a bowl.

❷ In a saucepan, combine the wine vinegar, sugar, and salt. Heat gently over a low flame until the sugar dissolves completely. Pour the mixture over the rice and fork through. Cover with a clean tea towel until cool enough to handle.

3 Spread the salmon with a little wasabi paste. Moisten your hands, and shape the cooled rice to the same shape as the fish. Place the salmon on top of the rice.

4 Serve with a bowl of soy sauce for dipping, and extra wasabi paste. Go slow on the wasabi—your lover might find it all too hot to handle...

Love can sometimes be magic. But magic can sometimes just be an illusion... (Javan Saying)

THE JAPANESE ARE ONE OF THE HEALTHIEST AND MOST LONG-LIVING RACES IN THE WORLD, WHICH IS IN PART DUE TO THEIR HIGH CONSUMPTION OF OILY FISH. SERVE THIS SEAFOOD DISH, WRAPPED IN SEAWEED OR ON ITS OWN, AS A HEALTHY ALTERNATIVE TO OTHER SNACKS.

Shrimps wrapped in a Blanket

Snuggle up together with these delicious little parcels. Soon you'll be wanting to unwrap each other all over again!

SERVES 2

What to buy

For the 'blanket':
- 125 g/4 ½ oz plain flour
- 1 egg
- 300 ml/ 10 fl oz milk
- 2 tbsp vegetable oil

For the filling:
- 2 tbsp olive oil
- 1 red onion, cut into wedges
- 1 courgette (zucchini), cut into chunks
- 1 red and 1 yellow (bell) pepper, seeded and cut into chunks
- 2 garlic cloves, crushed
- 225 g/8 oz can tomatoes
- 2 tbsp sun-dried tomato purée
- 225 g/8 oz (prawns) shrimps, cooked and peeled

- 8 tbsp crème fraîche
- 50 g/2 oz Cheddar cheese, grated
- A handful fresh basil leaves, chopped

How to cook it

THESE CRÊPES ARE FULL OF GOODNESS. BOTH EGGS AND PRAWNS (SHRIMPS) ARE PROTEIN-PACKED, WHILE THE VEGETABLES ADD PLENTY OF VITAMINS AND MINERALS. A DELICIOUS SNACK THAT WILL GIVE YOU NEW ENERGIES AND LOTS OF STAYING POWER, FOR HAPPY MOMENTS TOGETHER.

❶ Sift the flour into a large bowl with a pinch of salt. Whisk in the egg, milk, and 1 tbsp oil to make a smooth batter. Cover and chill for 20 minutes.
❷ Meanwhile, make the filling. Heat the oil and fry the onion, courgette (zucchini) and (bell) peppers for 3-4 minutes until softened. Stir in the garlic, tomatoes, and purée. Bring to the boil and simmer for 10 minutes. Add the shrimps and simmer for a further 5 minutes. Season and stir in the basil.
❸ Make the blankets: coat the base of a 20 cm/8 in frying pan with oil. Swirl in enough batter to coat base of pan. Cook over a moderate heat for 2 minutes, flipping once. Repeat and make 8 crêpes. Stack, interleaved with greaseproof paper.
❹ Heat the grill to hot. Place filling in center of each crêpe. Fold to make a parcel. Place the crêpes in a heat-proof dish. Dot with the crème fraîche, black pepper and cheese. Grill for 3 minutes and serve.
❺ Now, snuggle up under a blanket in front of the fire and enjoy these seductive little shrimp parcels together.

Silky Smooth Dip

**This passionate salsa made with aubergine (eggplant) will stimulate
all the senses—so don't eat it if all you want to do is sleep!**

SERVES 2

What to buy

- 225 g/8 oz aubergines (eggplant), diced
- 1 tbsp oil
- 2 tsp dried chili flakes
- 1 ½ tbsp soy sauce
- 1 tbsp rice vinegar or sherry
- 1 tsp sugar
- ½ tsp sesame oil
- ½ onion, thinly sliced
- A selection of fresh vegetables to dip,
  including broccoli florets, carrot sticks,
  celery, and (bell) peppers, cut into strips

How to cook it

❶ Place the aubergine (eggplant)
dice into a colander over a saucepan
of simmering water, and cook for
about 15 minutes, or until softened.
Drain and set aside.

❷ In a small frying pan, heat the oil.
Add the chili flakes and cook for
about 30 seconds. Remove from the
heat and stir in the soy sauce, vinegar,
sugar, and sesame oil. Pour the
mixture over the aubergine
(eggplant). Cover and chill for about
30 minutes in the refrigerator.

3 Stir the sliced onion into the aubergine (eggplant) mixture, and check the seasoning.

4 Serve with a variety of crunchy vegetables to dip, and with some bread sticks or hot pitta bread. Pour a glass of red wine, and let love and lust take over.

A good cook is like a sorceress who dispenses happiness...
(Elsa Schiaparelli)

Crunch-time

THIS VELVETY DIP WITH CRUNCHY VEGETABLES IS AN IDEAL IN-BETWEEN SNACK. THE ANCIENT GREEKS ALREADY KNEW HOW SEXY CARROTS COULD BE, AND ATE THEM IN PREPARATION FOR ORGIES. AND AUBERGINES (EGGPLANTS) WERE KNOWN AS 'APPLES OF LOVE' IN INDIA—THE KAMA SUTRA RECOMMENDS RUBBING THEIR JUICE OVER YOUR PARTNER'S BODY TO INCREASE SEXUAL DESIRE...

Pep-up-your-Lovelife Pizza

If passion's fires are burning low, turn up the wick again with this Italian classic. It's hot in every sense!

SERVES 2

What to buy

- 4 tbsp olive oil
- 1 bunch spring onions (scallions), trimmed and chopped
- 225 g/8 oz mushrooms
- 2 garlic cloves, crushed
- Salt and pepper
- 1 pizza base, about 25-30 cm/10-12 in diameter
- 20 slices pepperoni
- 1 small can sweetcorn kernels, drained
- 4 tbsp freshly grated Parmesan cheese
- Thyme sprigs, to garnish

How to cook it

❶ Preheat the oven to 220°C/425°F/ Gas Mark 7. Heat 2 tbsp of the oil in a frying pan. Add the spring onions (scallions), mushrooms, and garlic and fry over a medium heat for about

5–10 minutes, or until all the juices have evaporated. Season to taste and leave to cool.

❷ Brush the pizza base with half the remaining oil. Arrange the pepperoni, mushroom mixture, and sweetcorn on top. Sprinkle over the Parmesan, then drizzle over the remaining oil. Bake for 15-20 minutes. Garnish with thyme and serve.

❸ Your lover's mouth will be watering and he'll be lusting after more—pizza and you!

Sex is good, but not as good as fresh sweetcorn... (Garrison Keillor)

Spice it up

PEPPERONI AND OTHER SPICY SAUSAGES CONTAINING PAPRIKA OR CHILI POWDER ADD FLAVOR TO YOUR FOOD AND SPICE TO YOUR LOVING. HOT SPICES ARE KNOWN TO CREATE FEEL-GOOD HORMONES IN THE BODY WHICH WILL MAKE YOU MORE CONFIDENT AND ADVENTUROUS...

Frisky Frittata with Peppers

Here's the perfect 'quickie' to satisfy that late-night hunger—so you can get straight back to the main course!

SERVES 2

What to buy

- 2 potatoes, peeled
- 1 tbsp olive oil
- 1 red (bell) pepper, seeded and sliced
- 1 green (bell) pepper, seeded and sliced
- 1 yellow (bell) pepper, seeded and sliced
- 1 onion, chopped
- 4 eggs
- Salt and pepper

How to cook it

❶ Cook the potatoes until just tender. Drain and cut in slices.

❷ In a large frying pan, heat the oil, and fry the (bell) peppers and onion for 5 minutes, or until softened. Stir occasionally, then add the potatoes and cook for 3-4 minutes more.

❸ Beat the eggs and season to taste with salt and pepper. Pour the eggs over the vegetables.

4 Cook for 1-2 minutes, then lift the edges of the frittata to let the unset egg run underneath. Cook for another 1-2 minutes, until it begins to brown.

5 Place a large plate on top of the pan, turn both over together, then let the frittata gently slide back into the pan, the same side up, so that the underside can be cooked. Fry for 2-3 minutes, until set.

6 Serve the frittata at once, with a glass of red wine, and feel how you're both getting frisky.

As life's pleasures go, food is second only to sex. Except for salami and eggs...
(Alan King)

Rich variations

EGGS ARE FULL OF B-VITAMINS. THEY WILL BLOW AWAY ANY BEDROOM BLUES AND HELP THE BODY COPE WITH STRESS. YOU COULD ALWAYS DOUBLE THE PASSION QUOTIENT BY REPLACING THE PEPPERS WITH TRUFFLES, WHICH ARE ALSO SAID TO INCREASE YOUR DESIRE...

Creamy Venison Goulash

A dream of a dish—and that's how your lover will look on you after tasting this mouth-watering feast.

SERVES 2

What to buy

- 15 g/½ oz dried chanterelle mushrooms
- 1 tbsp vegetable oil
- 1 onion, roughly chopped
- 100 g/4 oz bacon, diced
- 300 g/11 oz venison steak
- 250 ml/8 fl oz/1 cup red wine
- 400 g/14 oz can peeled tomatoes
- 1 bay leaf
- 3 juniper berries, crushed
- Salt and pepper
- 4 tbsp crème fraîche

How to cook it

1 Soak the dried mushrooms for 15 minutes in hot water. Heat the oil in a large saucepan and fry the onion for 5 minutes until transparent. Add the bacon and fry, stirring.

2 Meanwhile, trim the venison, cut the meat into bite-sized pieces, add to the pan and fry, stirring, until browned on all sides.

3 Drain the mushrooms, then add to the pan, together with half the red wine and the tomatoes. Stir to combine, squashing the tomatoes.

❹ Add the bay leaf and juniper berries and season. Reduce the heat, cover with a lid, and simmer gently for 30 minutes. Remove the bay leaf.
❺ Add the remaining wine, check the seasoning, and cook for a further 15 minutes.
❻ To serve, transfer to individual plates and stir in the crème fraîche. Serve with a chilled bottle of Pinot Noir for some classy romance.

The act of putting into your mouth what the earth has grown is perhaps the most direct interaction with the earth...
(Frances Morre Lapp)

Naughty Nutty Nibbles

If your ardor is cooling, these naughty nuggets will bring you back to the boil!

MAKES 1

What to buy

- 2 tbsp vegetable oil
- 2 onions, finely chopped
- 1 garlic clove, crushed
- 225 g/8 oz walnuts (or other nuts such as hazel or Brazil nuts), finely chopped
- 75 g/3 oz fresh breadcrumbs
- 2 tsp fresh mixed herbs, chopped
- 1 tbsp mild curry powder
- 1 green (bell) pepper, seeded and finely chopped
- 225 g/8 oz tomatoes, peeled and chopped
- 1 egg, beaten
- Salt and pepper

How to cook it

1 Preheat the oven to 220°C/425°F/ Gas Mark 7. Heat the oil in a frying pan and gently fry the onion and garlic for about 5 minutes, or until they are softened.

2 Meanwhile, combine the nuts and breadcrumbs in a large bowl. Add the herbs and the curry powder. Stir in the onion-garlic mixture, (bell) pepper, and tomatoes, mix thoroughly.

and season. Add the beaten egg and
stir in to bind.

❸ Fill the mixture into a greased
18 cm/7 in square cake tin and bake
for 30-40 minutes, or until golden.

❹ Serve, cut into bite-sized squares,
with a glass of full-bodied red wine.
Now start nibbling away. Earlobes are
a good place to start…

Naughty nuts

THE ANCIENT ROMANS KNEW
ABOUT THE SAUCY EFFECT OF
WALNUTS—THEY NAMED THEM
'JUGLANS', MEANING THE GLANS
OF JUPITER! AT MARRIAGE
CEREMONIES, THE ROMANS
THREW WALNUTS INSTEAD OF
RICE (OUCH, SAID THE BRIDE),
AND IN FRANCE AND ITALY,
TOO, WALNUT PREPARATIONS
HAVE BEEN USED TO INCREASE
DESIRE…

Lust is when you love
what you see, love is
when you lust for
what's inside…
(Anon)

Passionate Potions

Passionate drinks for passionate people—these 'magic' potions will get your juices flowing again!

Purple Passion

- 4 parts vodka
- 8 parts red grape juice
- 8 parts grapefruit juice
- Plenty of crushed ice

1 In a cocktail shaker, combine all the ingredients with crushed ice and shake vigorously.
2 Pour into chilled cocktail glasses and down in one passionate slurp.

Grand Passion

- 2 parts gin
- 2 parts dry vermouth
- 2 parts passion fruit syrup
- 1 part fresh lemon juice
- A twist of orange zest
- Plenty of crushed ice

1 In a cocktail shaker, combine all the ingredients with crushed ice and shake vigorously.
2 Pour into chilled cocktail glasses and garnish with the orange twist.

Passionate Daiquiri

- 4 parts white rum
- 2 parts lime juice
- 1 part passion fruit syrup
- Plenty of crushed ice

❶ In a cocktail shaker, combine all the ingredients with crushed ice and shake vigorously.
❷ Pour into chilled cocktail glasses and let the orgy begin.

Sex is two plus two making five, rather than four...
(Marty Feldman)

Liquid bread

ANCIENT ROMAN WRITERS KNEW WELL THAT ALCOHOLIC DRINKS COULD GET YOU GOING! AS ONE WROTE, 'WITHOUT CERES (BREAD) AND LIBERO (WINE) VENUS (LOVE) WILL FREEZE.' HOWEVER, IT WAS ALSO NOTED THAT EXCESSES COULD HINDER RATHER THAN HELP. SO DON'T OVERDO IT BEFORE YOU'VE HAD SOME FUN...

According to one scientific study, the consumption of alcohol has been observed to raise the testosterone level in women. And, so say the researchers, 'additional small amounts can dramatically increase the libido. For women who lack sexual interest and desire, the treatment can be life-changing'. Well, let's go for some treatment then...

Get a mouth full

AS WE ALL KNOW, ALCOHOL WILL REDUCE ANXIETY AND RELEASE INHIBITIONS—HENCE THE NUMBER OF DANGEROUS LIAISONS AFTER OFFICE PARTIES! WATCH OUT, THOUGH, BECAUSE IT'S VERY EASY TO (A) SUCCUMB TO ITS SEDATIVE EFFECTS—YOU'LL JUST FALL ASLEEP, OR (B) SAY THE WRONG THING TO THE RIGHT PERSON...

Bedtime Beverages

These carnal cocktails are named for a good reason. Drink them and you'll be stirred, not shaken!

Between the Sheets

- 4 parts brandy or cognac
- 3 parts white rum
- 1 part white Curaçao
- 1 part fresh lemon juice
- Plenty of crushed ice

1 In a cocktail shaker, combine all the ingredients with crushed ice and shake vigorously.
2 Pour into chilled cocktail glasses and slip between your own sheets.

One Exciting Night

- 1 dash of orange juice
- 1 part dry vermouth
- 1 part sweet vermouth
- 1 part gin
- Plenty of crushed ice

1 Moisten the rim of a port glass or round wine glass and dip into caster (superfine) sugar.
2 Shake the ingredients well with ice and strain into this glass. Decorate with a twist of lemon peel and serve, to start your own exciting night...

chapter

4

Irresistible desserts t
make your honey act o
your every whim

Sweet Seduction

Sweets for your
sweet, sugar for
your honey...

contents

Honey and Cream Figs — 77

Forbidden Fruit Salad — 78

Nights in White Satin — 80

Passionate Fruit Cups — 83

Wickedly Seductive Marbled Cake — 84

Sticky Peaches — 86

Apple Tart with Gently
Whipped Cream — 88

Potent Pumpkin Cookies — 90

Loving Lavender Syllabub — 92

Coffee Liqueur Restorers — 94

Honey and Cream Figs

Only your lover could be sweeter than this velvety dessert.

Sheer bliss!

SERVES 2

What to buy

- 250 g/9 oz fresh figs
- 50 g/2 oz dark chocolate
- 250 g/9 oz ricotta cheese
- Zest of 1 orange
- 2 tbsp clear honey

How to make it

❶ Halve the figs crossways, keeping the corresponding halves together.

❷ Roughly chop or break up the chocolate. Place in a bowl with the ricotta and orange zest. Stir well.

❸ Using a teaspoon, carefully place a spoonful of the ricotta mixture onto the bottom half of each fig. Replace the top half of the fig and place the figs on a serving plate.

❹ Drizzle the honey over the figs and share a lovin' spoonful.

Forbidden Fruit Salad

Transport your baby to paradise with this voluptuous whirl of fruity sensations. So sweet it's sinful!

SERVES 2

What to buy

For the syrup:
- 125 ml/4 fl oz ginger wine
- 50 g/2 oz caster (superfine) sugar
- 2 passion fruits, halved

For the fruit salad:
- ½ pineapple
- 1 mango
- 1 dessert apple
- 1 kiwi fruit
- A handful of summer berries (raspberries, blueberries, or strawberries)
- 1 orange, peeled and segmented
- 225 g/8 oz canned lychees, drained and halved

How to make it

❶ Make the syrup: put the ginger wine and sugar into a saucepan. Bring to the boil over a medium heat. Turn off the heat, and add the passion fruit pulp, juice, and seeds. Leave to infuse and cool completely while you prepare the fruit salad.

❷ Prepare the fruit: cut the hard skin off the pineapple and remove the core. Halve and peel the mango, and remove the stone. Peel the apple, quarter, and core. Peel the kiwi fruit. ❸ Cut all the fruit into bite-sized pieces and put them into a large bowl. Pour over the syrup and gently toss the fruits. Leave to marinate for at least 10 minutes before serving. ❹ Heaven can wait, but your honey needs you now.

The soul that can speak with its eyes can also kiss with a gaze... (Anon)

Juicy, fruity...

A PERFECTLY RIPE PIECE OF FRUIT SHARED WITH YOUR LOVER IS A TRUE ROMANTIC MOMENT. FRUITS ARE HEALTHY, DELICIOUSLY MOUTH-WATERING, AND PACKED WITH THE VITAMINS OF LOVE. WHY ELSE WOULD EVE HAVE CHOSEN TO SEDUCE ADAM WITH AN APPLE?

Nights in White Satin

This elegant dessert is snow-white and inviting—just like smooth, satin sheets...

SERVES 4

What to buy

- 100 g/4 oz white chocolate
- 225 ml/8fl oz/1 cup single (light) cream
- 1 tsp caster (superfine) sugar
- 1 egg yolk
- 1 tbsp kirsch
- 1 tbsp sugar

How to make it

1 Break the chocolate into pieces, put them into a bowl together with the sugar and 2 tbsp of the cream, and place the bowl over a saucepan of gently simmering water to melt the chocolate.

2 In a separate bowl, also set over a saucepan of simmering water, beat together the egg yolk, kirsch, and 1 tbsp water, until you have a pale, creamy mixture.

3 Take both mixtures off the heat, and gently fold the melted chocolate into the egg-kirsch mixture. Leave the mixture to cool until lukewarm.

4 Beat the remaining cream with a hand-held whisk until stiff. Using a rubber spatula, quickly fold the whipped cream into the chocolate mixture in figures of eight.

5 Fill the mixture into a shallow dish, cover with clingfilm (plastic wrap), and chill for at least 1 hour in the fridge.

6 Dip a large dessert spoon into hot water, then use to spoon out the chocolate. Share this super-elegant chocolate mousse in bed—it's white, so no worries about the sheets...

I think there's danger in overexposure. Just think what happened to Lady Godiva—she became a chocolate...
(Kenneth Jay Lane)

Eat it, wear it

CHOCOLATE HAS ALWAYS BEEN KNOWN AS *THE* SEXY FOOD, AND IT IS MORE POPULAR THAN EVER—CHOCOLATE BODY PAINT IS A FAVORITE PRESENT, AND RECENTLY, A PARIS DESIGNER WOWED A CONFECTIONERY FAIR WITH MODELS DRESSED ONLY IN CHOCOLATE LINGERIE!

Fruits of Passion

You can use any number of different fruits to float in this Champagne cup. Mangoes, for example, are good anti-depressants and ancient Indians believed them to prolong love making. Meanwhile strawberries have been found to increase your ability to perform…

Ugly but nice

PASSION FRUITS ARE A NATIVE OF BRAZIL, BUT THEY ARE NOW GROWN IN AUSTRALIA, AMERICA, AND AFRICA, AND ARE AVAILABLE ALL YEAR ROUND. CHOOSE LARGE, HEAVY FRUIT WITH DEEP PURPLE SKINS. ALTHOUGH THEY DO NOT LOOK VERY PROMISING, YOU'LL FIND A CLUSTER OF DELICIOUSLY SWEET, YELLOWY GREEN SEEDS UNDER THEIR WRINKLY SKINS.

Passionate Fruit Cups

Scale the heights of passion with this sparkling dessert. Make it as fruity as you like!

SERVES 4-6

What to buy

- 300 ml/10 fl oz fresh orange juice
- 150 ml/5fl oz grape juice
- 1 liter/35 fl oz passion fruit juice
- 4 passion fruits, halved
- A selection of fresh fruits
- 1 bottle Champagne or sparkling wine

How to cook it

1 Chill all the fruit juices for at least 30 minutes. Pour the chilled juices together into a large bowl just before you are ready to serve. Stir to mix. Stir in the pulp and seeds of the passion fruits.

2 Prepare the fresh fruit. Use, for example, peeled and sliced kiwi fruit, peeled and sliced mangoes, hulled strawberries, raspberries, seedless grapes, unwaxed lemon slices. Float all the prepared fruit on top of the juices in the bowl.

3 Pour over the Champagne or sparkling wine, help yourself to a cup, and pull your baby into your lovin' arms for some smooching.

Wickedly Seductive Marbled Cake

This chilled confection is sheer perfection! The perfect end to a perfect meal—and the rest of the night awaits.

MAKES 1

What to buy

- 100 g/4 oz pecan nuts
- 100 g/4 oz dried apricots
- 150 g/5 oz porridge oats
- 25 g/1 oz rice krispies
- 25 g/1 oz bran flakes, lightly crushed
- 75 g/3 oz raisins
- 1 tsp molasses syrup
- 150 ml/5 fl oz whole condensed milk
- 150 g/5 oz dark chocolate, broken into small pieces
- 150 g/5 oz white chocolate, broken into small pieces

How to make it

1 Heat the oven to 180°C/350°F/ Gas Mark 4. Toast and chop the pecan nuts. Chop the apricots. In a bowl mix together the oats, rice krispies, bran flakes, apricots, pecans, and raisins.

❷ In a small saucepan, heat the molasses and milk until warm and thoroughly blended, then pour this mixture into the bowl with the fruits and nuts. Mix with a wooden spoon.

❸ Tip the mixture into a 15 x 25 x 2.5 cm/6 x 10 x 1 in deep non-stick baking tin, pressing it down evenly. Bake in the oven for 25 minutes, or until golden brown. Remove and leave to cool completely.

❹ Meanwhile, melt the dark and white chocolates in separate bowls set over pans of simmering water. When the cereal mixture has cooled, turn it out onto a board. Spoon the dark chocolate over the top of the cake, leaving spaces between each spoonful. Then do the same with the white chocolate, filling in the gaps.

❺ With a small palette knife, in a zigzag motion, swirl both chocolates together to give a marbled effect. Gently tap the board to create a smooth finish. Chill the cake for about 1 hour before slicing and serving.

❻ Serve ice-cold, and seduce your darling with hot kisses.

Sensual crumbs

CHOCOLATE CONTAINS METHYLXANTHINES WHICH STIMULATE THE TRANSMISSION AND CONDUCTION OF NERVE IMPULSES—IN OTHER WORDS, THEY CREATE A FEELING OF WELL-BEING. AND IF THAT'S NOT ENOUGH TO GET YOU GOING, THE OATS IN THIS CAKE INCREASE TESTOSTERONE LEVELS, PUMPING UP THE LIBIDO. SO MAKE SURE YOU GET YOUR OATS...

Sticky Peaches

Sweet, succulent and bursting with juice—these sensual fruit are a perfect prelude to passion à deux.

SERVES 2

What to buy

- 2 ripe peaches, skinned
- Grated zest and juice of ½ orange
- 40 g/1 ½ oz gingernut biscuits (gingersnaps), crushed
- 25 g/1 oz mixed nuts, chopped
- 25 g/1 oz light brown sugar
- 25 g/1 oz butter
- 1 egg yolk
- 1 tsp runny honey
- Mint leaves, to decorate
- Greek yogurt, to serve

How to cook it

❶ Cut the peaches in half and remove stones. Trim their bases so they sit without rocking. Dip each peach half in orange juice, then place in a large heavy-based frying pan.

❷ Put the gingernuts (gingersnaps) into a bowl and add the nuts, sugar, orange zest, and butter. Work with your fingertips until the mixture resembles breadcrumbs. Mix in the egg yolk to make it all stick together.

❸ Divide the crumb mixture between the peaches and press into the peach cavity. Add 4 tbsp water to the pan, cover and cook over a very low heat for about 15 minutes, or until the peaches are tender. Heat the grill.

4 Transfer to a hot grill for about 5 minutes to brown the filling. Drizzle the honey over the peaches. Garnish with mint and serve in the pan, with Greek yogurt.

5 Get sticky all over—your kisses will never taste the same again!

Sex stops when you pull up your pants, Love never lets you go...
(Kingsley Amis)

The sticky stuff

HONEY IS RICH IN BORON, A MINERAL THAT IS SAID TO HELP THE BODY ABSORB FEMALE SEX HORMONES AND TO INCREASE LEVELS OF THE MALE SEX HORMONES. THE EFFECT IS EARTH-SHATTERING: A GREATER INTEREST IN SEX, MORE STAMINA, AND MORE ENJOYMENT FROM IT...

Apple Tart with Gently Whipped Cream

Whip up the passions with this tantalizing tart—your honey will soon be begging you for more!

MAKES 1

What to buy

- 1 kg/2 ¼ lb dessert apples, peeled, cored and sliced
- 100 g/4 oz caster (superfine) sugar
- 150 ml/5 fl oz cider
- 500 g/1lb 2oz puff pastry
- 1 tbsp cornflour (cornstarch)
- Icing (confectioner's) sugar, for dusting
- Whipped cream, to serve
- Vanilla essence for flavoring

How to make it

1 Heat the oven to 200°C/400°F/ Gas Mark 6. Sprinkle apples with caster (superfine) sugar. Pour over the cider. Cover with clingfilm (plastic wrap), and set aside.

2 Divide the pastry into three equal portions. Roll out and cut into circles,

25 cm/10 in in diameter. Place the pastry circles on baking trays dampened with water and bake for 15-20 minutes, until cooked and lightly browned. Cool on wire racks.

❸ In a saucepan, slowly bring the apple and the cider to the boil, lower heat and simmer for 5 minutes. Drain, reserving 150 ml/5 fl oz of the cooking liquid.

❹ Mix the cornflour (cornstarch) with a little water and add to the reserved liquid. Place the mixture in a pan and bring to the boil until thickened, stirring. Add the drained apples and coat in the mixture. Remove from the heat and leave to cool slightly.

❺ Put one pastry circle on a serving plate; arrange half the apple slices on top. Cover with a second pastry circle and arrange the rest of the apple slices on this. Top with the third circle and dust with icing (confectioner's) sugar.

❻ Whip the cream, flavor it with a few drops of vanilla essence and serve. Go on: have another slice!

Deliciously light

THIS PUFF-PASTRY TART IS FEATHER-LIGHT, JUST THE RIGHT THING TO SHARE WITH YOUR HONEYBUN. THERE'S NOTHING WORSE THAN FEELING FULL OR BLOATED WHEN YOU'RE JUST ABOUT TO EMBARK ON SOME FUN AND GAMES—KEEP IT LIGHT!

Potent Pumpkin Cookies

Pumpkins aren't just for Hallowe'en—treat your lover to these delicious cookies, and you won't need any 'tricks' to get them up the stairs!

MAKES 30

What to buy

- 125 g/4 ½ oz butter, softened
- 150 g/5 oz plain (all-purpose) flour
- 175 g/6 oz soft light brown sugar
- 225 g/8 oz cooked pumpkin
- 1 egg, beaten
- 2 tsp ground cinnamon
- 2 ½ tsp vanilla essence
- ½ tsp baking powder
- ½ tsp grated nutmeg
- 125 g/4 ½ oz wholemeal (whole-wheat) flour
- 75 g/3 oz pecan nuts, roughly chopped
- 100 g/4 oz raisins
- 50 g/2 oz unsalted butter
- 225 g/8 oz sugar
- 2 tbsp milk

How to make them

❶ Heat the oven to 190°C/375°F/ Gas Mark 5. Grease a baking sheet.

❷ Beat the butter until light and fluffy. Add the flour, sugar, pumpkin, and egg, and mix. Stir in the cinnamon, 1 tsp vanilla essence; sift in the baking powder and the nutmeg. Beat until combined well.

❸ Add the wholemeal (whole-wheat) flour, chopped nuts, and raisins to the mixture and fold in.

❹ Place teaspoons of the mixture, about 5cm/2in apart, on the baking sheet. Bake in the oven for 10-12 minutes, or until the edges are firm.

❺ Remove the cookies from the oven and leave to cool on a wire rack. Meanwhile, melt the butter in a small saucepan over a medium heat, until pale and just turning golden. Remove from heat. Add the sugar, remaining vanilla essence and milk, stirring.

❻ Drizzle over the cookies and serve with a cup of steaming coffee. Keep the curtains drawn and the doors firmly closed!

Does size matter?

ONE OF THE LARGEST FRUITS AROUND, CHAMPIONSHIP PUMPKINS CAN WEIGH **800** POUNDS OR MORE, GROWING SOME **10–15** POUNDS PER DAY! ALTHOUGH THERE ARE MANY DELICIOUS RECIPES USING PUMPKIN, 99% ARE SOLD FOR DECORATIVE USE AT HALLOWEEN.

Loving Lavender Syllabub

Stimulate all your lover's senses with this fragrant dessert—a perfect climax to any meal!

SERVES 4-6

What to buy

For the syllabub:
- 150 ml/5 fl oz white wine
- 2-3 fresh lavender spikes
- 2 tbsp caster (superfine) sugar
- Juice of 1 lemon
- 1 tbsp eau-de-vie or brandy
- 300 ml/½ pint/10 fl oz chilled double (heavy) cream

For the caramel:
- 3 tbsp caster sugar
- 1 tsp fresh lavender flowers

How to cook it

❶ Heat the wine in a small pan, removing it just before it comes to the boil and add the lavender spikes. Leave to infuse for 10 minutes, strain, and stir in the sugar, lemon juice, and eau-de-vie or brandy. Whisk the cream until it begins to hold its shape, whisk in the lavender-wine infusion, and chill in the fridge.

❷ Meanwhile, make the caramel. Heat a heavy frying pan over a medium heat, and sprinkle in the sugar. Watch carefully as it melts and then caramelizes—don't let it burn. As it cooks shake the pan every now and then to distribute the crystals evenly, but do not stir. As soon as the sugar melts to a warm brown, remove from the heat and stir in the lavender flowers. Pour onto a lightly oiled plate, and leave to cool and set.

❸ Once hardened, place the caramel between two sheets of clingfilm (plastic wrap), break it into small pieces with a rolling pin. Fold these into the syllabub just before serving.

❹ Lusty kisses and loving arms—is there no end to the beneficial effects of lavender?

Coffee Liqueur Restorers

Hot and fresh, with a dash of spirit—that's how you'll feel after one of these perfect late-night revivers!

Amaretto Coffee

- 3 parts Amaretto liqueur
- 1 cup of hot freshly made coffee
- Ground coriander (cilantro)
- Whipped cream

❶ Pour the Amaretto into the coffee and stir to combine.
❷ Sprinkle with the coriander (cilantro) and serve with whipped cream.

I feel the end approaching. Quick, bring me my dessert, coffee and liqueur...
(Brillat-Savarin's Greataunt Pierette)

Black Magic

- 4 parts vodka
- 2 parts coffee liqueur
- A dash of freshly squeezed lemon juice

1 Combine the vodka, coffee liqueur and lemon juice in a large glass and stir well.

2 To serve, strain over ice cubes into a chilled whisky tumbler and quickly cast a spell on your lover.

The mind is the most potent aphrodisiac there is...
(Anon)

Caffeine fix

COFFEE IS A POWERFUL STIMULANT THAT CAN OVERCOME FATIGUE AND INCREASE MENTAL ALERTNESS WHEN YOU ARE FEELING LOW. SO IF YOU'RE AFTER A LONG NIGHT OF PASSIONATE EMBRACES, JUST HAVE A QUICK PICK-ME-UP BEFORE HITTING THE SHEETS...

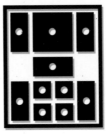